# REALLY EASY JAZZIN' A
## fun pieces for
## OBOE

## CONTENTS

© 2002 by Faber Music Ltd
First published in 2002 by Faber Music Ltd
Bloomsbury House 74–77 Great Russell Street London WC1B 3DA
Cover by Velladesign
Music processed by Don Sheppard
Printed in England by Caligraving Ltd
All rights reserved

ISBN10: 0-571-52124-X
EAN13: 978-0-571-52124-1

# PAM WEDGWOOD

FABER _ff_ MUSIC

# Tangerine

Pam Wedgwood

**With a good steady beat** ♩ = 104

*to Debbie*

# Dragonfly

# Easy tiger

# Riding out west

D.S.𝄋 al ⊕
poi al Coda

**CODA**

# Smooth operator

# Wrap it up

# Hot chilli

# Crystal spring

# Keep truckin'

# Buttercup

# Cat walk

# Cheeky cherry